When Silence Blooms

Supriya Ghaytadak

BookLeaf
Publishing

India | USA | UK

To Mammi and Pappa,

who first placed a pencil and slate in my hand

*and taught me that words can be both shelter
and wings.*

Thank you for patiently tracing every word,

gently shaping every sentence,

and believing in my voice even before I knew

it was mine.

And to my little brother,

*the brightest star in my sky, who has been my
steady anchor and my greatest joy.*

This book, and all the words within,

exist because of you.

Acknowledgement

This collection is a tapestry woven from moments and memories I usually keep to myself. As an introvert, sharing doesn't come naturally to me. These poems are pieces of my heart that found their way onto the page during sleepless nights. I'm deeply grateful to everyone who has been part of this journey, listening patiently as I slowly found the courage to put these words on the page.

To my friends, Saurabh Bhuwania and Pourush, who patiently listened to my endless thoughts, even the wildly irrational ones and still encouraged me, thank you. Your unwavering support (and remarkable tolerance) means the world to me.

To my brother from another mother, Prasenjeet, who designed the cover with endless patience and artistic flair, thank you for bringing my words to life. Your presence through the chaos has been invaluable.

My heartfelt thanks to BookLeaf Publishing for guiding my words from the page to print, and breathing life into this collection.

To all the readers who find pieces of themselves within these pages, I hope these poems touch your heart as deeply as writing them has touched mine. May they remind you of the beauty in both sorrow and joy, the strength in vulnerability, and the magic in quiet moments.

And finally, to the poets, authors, and dreamers who came before me and left a trail of words to follow, thank you for inspiring me to find my own voice.

With deepest gratitude,
Supriya Ghaytadak

Preface

Poetry has always held a special place in my life. My mother possesses a rare talent for weaving magic into every line she writes, her words flowing effortlessly from pen to paper. Growing up, I would watch her craft beautiful verses as if language itself were her canvas and she, the artist. Often, I found myself wondering, "Where did those poetic genes go?" No matter how many times I tried, my own attempts felt clumsy— what I saw as a disastrous addition to the history of poetry.

Even as a toddler, I couldn't help but admire her work. One of my earliest memories of poetry dates back to when I was just three and a half years old. In her notebook, I scribbled a little review—perhaps my first literary critique: "छान छान कविता, सुंदर अक्षर, खुप छान" (Nice poem, nice handwriting, very good). Back then, I took my role as her tiny poetry reviewer very seriously.

Over the years, I've come to realize that it's perfectly fine not to inherit all the same gifts as one's parents. After all, my parents taught my sibling and me to stay true to ourselves, never attempting to mould us into reflections of themselves. They encouraged us to explore our unique interests, no matter how different they might be.

The poem "Path of Light" came into existence in 2020 when I was asked (rather forced) to participate in the "Hindi Pakhwada Poetry Competition" on behalf of our batch, despite my failed protests. To my surprise, it ended up winning a Consolation Prize! That unexpected win marked my journey with poetry— a journey of expression, discovery and a growing love for words.

As I share this collection, each piece holds a fragment of my heart—a step towards finding my own voice and exploring expression through words. Within these pages, I hope you'll catch glimpses of this path, winding and unexpected, and perhaps find moments that stir something familiar in your own heart. May these poems kindle reflections, spark discoveries, and invite a deep connection between us, softly woven, word by word.

Supriya Ghaytadak

CONTENTS

Summer of 99

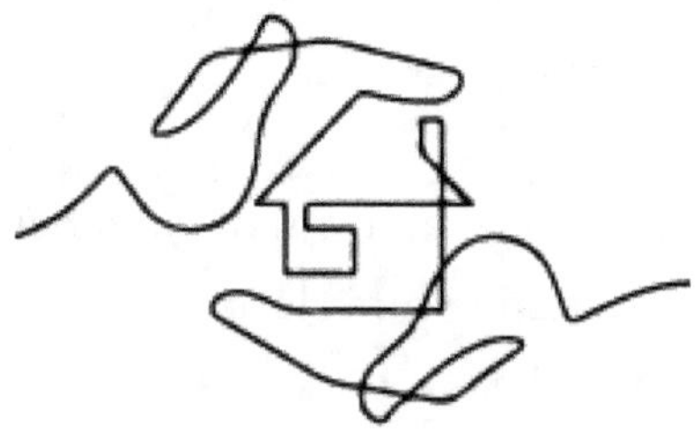

The blue window opens, and a warm summer
breeze enters the house.
Curtains flutter like whispers of forgotten
dreams,
A feng shui bell chimes softly, echoing in the
stillness.
She breathes in the fresh summer air
and looks around—
The house is just the same as it was when she
left.

The books rest quietly on the corner shelf.
She wonders if they remember her gentle
touch.
The tablecloth is just as tidy as it was,
an emblem of care.

And though the flowers aren't fresh, it's
okay—
Life persists in its own quiet way.
She doesn't complain.

The dog just woke up from his slumber.
She loves watching him sleep,
Such an angel he is
He taught her what unconditional love looks
like—
a bond that transcends words,
filling the spaces of her heart.

She listens carefully to her mother humming
in the backyard.
She pays attention to her father, immersed in
the newspaper.
Her brother is playing with his toys,
His laughter floats through the air.
It takes her mind back to the summer of '99,
A tapestry of memories stitched with
innocence and wonder.

Life looks simple and calm at home,
each corner a keeper of stories.
She thinks and thinks,
Perhaps she shouldn't have left the home.
In this stillness, she feels the pull of
belonging—
The gravity of love woven through the walls,
A reminder that sometimes, the journey leads
us back.

If I Could Meet My Mother in Time

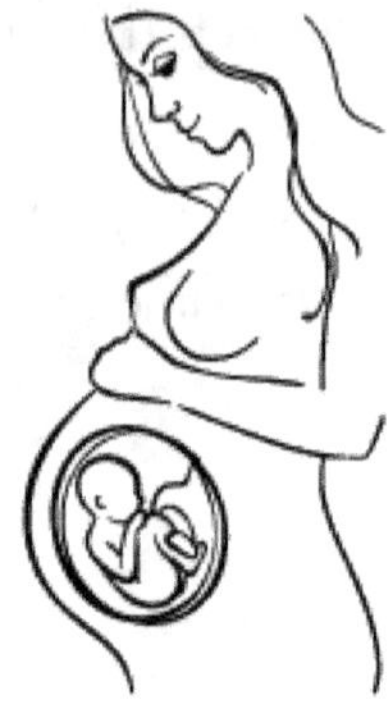

In another universe, I meet my mother as a
baby.
It's love at first sight—
her dusky skin, her wide, curious eyes.
I hold her tiny hands and promise,
"I will care for you forever."

I carry her on my shoulders, listening to her
endless chatter.
I ask if she's afraid of the monsters beneath
her bed
and never judge her words, for she's just a
baby,
still untouched by the world's harshness.
I tell her it's okay to be scared.

Years later, I meet her again in her teenage
bloom,
brimming with dreams and unspoken desires.
I want to ask her what she hopes to become,
to make her swear she'll never give up.
I beg her not to lose her spark,
to always follow the whispers of her heart,
no matter how loud the world gets.

Then I see her again, a woman now,
married to a man she barely knows.
She speaks little, her silence heavy with things
left unsaid.

I wonder if she ever loved,
if her heart was once woven into the wrong
hands,
if someone ever shattered her world.
I want to offer her my shoulders again.

She tells me she's happy,
but her eyes avoid mine.
She says it's alright, being the housewife, the
obedient daughter-in-law,
because that's what good women do—
they sacrifice their dreams to fit inside the
walls of tradition.

I want to go back in time. .
I want to protect her heart and dreams.
If only I could meet my mother in time.

If only I could meet her again in another life,
where she isn't bound by the weight of
silence,
where she laughs freely and chases the sky—
a world where love doesn't ask her to shrink
or hide.

I would stand beside her, a guardian of her dreams,
and whisper, "You are free to be anything, anything, but silent!"

Where Pages Breathe

I open the attic, and the dust lifts slow,
like the weight of time, of what I don't know.
How worn pages smell of times spent alone,
of whispered secrets the past has sown.
It's the scent of musty tales, of a childhood
spent chasing words and worlds,
of lonely magic resting on library shelves.

Where ink-stained dreams call like old
friends,
and adventures wait for the heart that
intends.
Each book, a portal to lands unexplored,
where heroes rise and legends are adored.
The stories breathe life into the shadows cast,
reminding me gently how these moments last.

With every page I read, I'm a traveler bold;
in the arms of these stories, I'll never grow
old.
In every library's corner, a beautiful magic
lies,
where each book holds a dream that never
dies.

Whispers of Autumn: Dreams, Shedding, and Silent Hopes

Summer is fading, and autumn sets in,
trees are shedding their leaves.
Untethered leaves finally touch the ground,
but the earth hasn't forgotten the warmth of
summer.
Each fallen leaf, a memory,
whispering stories of days gone by.

The sun sets, spreading orange-pink hues
across the canvas of the sky.
It's a cool, breezy evening.
A little plant stands at the crossroads,
uncertain of how tall it will grow.
It dreams of birds dancing and singing on its
arms,
of playful winds caressing its tender leaves.
It is too young to understand the pain of
shedding.

The moon peeks from behind gray, fluffy
clouds.
It's evening finally,
Trees stand stunned,
caught in the bittersweet moment of letting
go,
wondering if they will sleep easily.
If the fallen leaves will forgive them
for not holding on just a little longer.
Does shedding the past count as heartbreak?
Is it okay to dream of new leaves yet?

When Words Refuse

In the thick air of unspoken moments,
words hang like heavy clouds,
muffled by the weight of what could have
been said
but wasn't.

Each heartbeat echoes a memory,
a whisper of dreams left unspoken,
filling the quiet with unfulfilled wishes,
like shadows dancing in the dim light—
flickering, hesitant, yet persistent.

There are times when one's heart
writes poetry in the solitude ,
where emotions blossom like wildflowers,
rising in the concrete fissures, untamed yet
beautiful.

The lips part, but the words retreat,
and in that silence, a world unfolds:
the weight of a hand not held,
the echo of laughter just out of reach,
the longing that lingers like an unfinished
song.

And so I sit,
wrapped in the comfort of quiet,
where silence speaks with a voice of its own.
The unexpressed feelings become a tapestry,
woven with strands of hope and sorrow.
It reminds me that some emotions
are too profound for speech.

Chronicles of Solitude

In the quiet of my study room,
I gather the dust of forgotten dreams.
I listen to the rhythm of my own heart,
trying to find peace in the pauses in between.

The chair creaks softly, like an old lover's sigh.
I float through memories of times gone by—
each one like a leaf in the autumn wind,
drifting gently, without hurry or end.

I drift through the pages of forgotten years,
where lessons wait, just beyond the reach of
my fears.
In this solitude, I find my space to breathe,
a canvas where silence allows me to believe.

The light shifts softly, casting shadows long
and wide.
Every corner of the room feels like a place to
hide.
As the ink spills freely on the pages, my
thoughts take flight,
shining in the dark, bringing words into the
light.

Here, in the stillness, I learn to see
the miracle that sets me free.
In this solitude, I'm never alone.
I am both the author and the peace—
I am my own home.

Letter to Pluto

Dear Pluto,
out there on the edges of a galaxy, where
sunrays barely reach,
you drift in quiet solitude, like a speck in the
darkness,
unfazed by the voices from Earth that
debated your worth—
as if a name or a label could ever change what
you are.

They called you a planet once, a proud ninth
companion,
and then, with a wave of science and
discoveries,
they said you no longer belong.

But you stayed, silent as stone,
spinning your path without pause or
complaint.

You did not bend to their rules or their
reasons,
don't clamor for titles or fitting in frames.
You simply exist— a mystery, cold and steady,
carving out your place in the vastness of
space,
unmoved by the standards we conjure on
Earth.

Perhaps that's your quiet defiance:
to be distant, unknown, yet wholly yourself,
holding your orbit in the dark, alone but not
lonely—
an emblem of all that refuses to shrink or
conform.

So, here's to you, Pluto.
You are a reminder to mortal souls that worth
needs no witness,
that to walk alone is sometimes strength,
and that even in solitude, there is light—
not from the sun, but from simply being
yourself.

Strength in Shadows

She sits in the corner in gatherings,
doesn't speak a word.
She has starry eyes, full of dreams,
they hold galaxies of untold stories,
and her heart is full of unheard songs.
She has seen life.

She talks and talks about life, beautiful little
things,
but only with those whose hearts know how
to sing.
She has travelled distances, lived in cities,
yet nobody knows how deep her scars run,
hidden beneath a veneer of grace.

She smiles at strangers and believes in
kindness.
She says, that's the only thing that can save
the world.
She has faith in humanity.

But does anyone know where those deep scars
come from?
Is she incredibly strong or merely pretending
to be?
Does anyone know what makes her strong—
responsibilities weighing heavy, or a world
turned cruel?
Nobody knows.

I remember, she said that she has met the
kindest souls,
but, when were the wolves kind in the
history?
Dressed in kindness, veiled in deceit?
Does anyone know?

The Recipe of a Strong Woman

"What is the recipe for a strong woman?"
asks a young girl, hand raised in a crowded
room.
She wonders, does her mother,
who endures in silence, wearing bruises like
unseen scars—qualify as strong, or merely
broken?

Not everyone is privileged to be heard when
they speak,
but does that make the silenced ones weak?

She reads of history, heroes and victories,
but isn't history written by the dominant
ones?
Did ordinary women ever get to carve their
names in stone,
or did they build quietly,
their strength left unsung, unknown?

She imagines them—
mothers, daughters, sisters, and wives,
shaping the world through their invisible
lives,
their sacrifices woven into each home,
unrecognized, uncelebrated, unsung and often
alone.

So, she asks again,
what makes a woman strong?
Is it loud victories, or endurance prolonged?
The courage to rise, even when unheard,
to carry dreams, though they remain deferred.

Hey there, my faraway dream

Hey there, my faraway dream,
across the miles, you are closer than it seems.
Though words unspoken hang in the air,
in the quiet nights, I feel you are there.
Oh, how I wish you knew.

In my dreams, I see your smile,
a hundred roads, a thousand miles,
and yet your laugh, so soft and free,
echoes in my mind and stays close to me.
If only you knew too.

I have held this love long inside my chest,
in letters written, that were never sent.
You are far away but feel so near,
as if the distance could easily disappear.
What if you feel it too?

and maybe one day, fate will say
that you and I will find a way,
to close the miles that lie between,
and make real this faraway dream.
Until then, I will hold on to you.

Path of Light

My world moves on wheels of suffocation and
rage,
Once my heart froze at injustice, now it
lingers not to engage.
And the darkness, it seems, never lifts away,
for the world keeps moving, day after day.

Terror strikes, blood is shed, horrors untold,
rape and slaughter, these stories unfold.
No longer do we sit in torment or despair,
for the world moves on, without a care.

And the world will move,
no matter who we are.
You, me, or anyone, our struggles won't go far.
I've learned this secret, plain to see,
the world spins on in its selfish spree.

And I, I watch it all in silent dismay,
still trying, stumbling, finding my way,
to walk the path that leads to light,
to absorb the dark, and spread the bright.

Penance of a Stone

I sit on the boulder,
He says nothing.
It's a regular boulder with no particular
shape,
It's black and has marks of the evolution—the
cracks and the pores.
I think the boulder has been through a lot.

Silence hums around us,
broken only by a faint rustling as the wind
slips through cracks in his weathered face.
I wonder how he sits like a saint doing his
penance.

Does the scorching heat, heavy downpour,
the chilly winter affect his willpower?
No one really knows.

I don't understand the geography of his scars,
each fissure defying laws of time and space,
but isn't that how people become quiet?
Carrying burdens that weigh heavy on the
soul,
yet finding peace in stillness,
a refuge from the storm.

I wonder if he has a lot to say,
and I doubt if anyone ever paused to
understand him,
to listen to the stories etched in his being?
Or maybe that's why he is silent, guarding
secrets in the heart of his being.
I wonder how the world looks through his
eyes.
Does he find the Moon and stars beautiful?

I sit on the boulder and blabber about my
problems,
I like his company, he doesn't judge me at all.
Maybe he understands me, that's why he is
quiet.
He must have been through a lot.

To the woman who lit my way

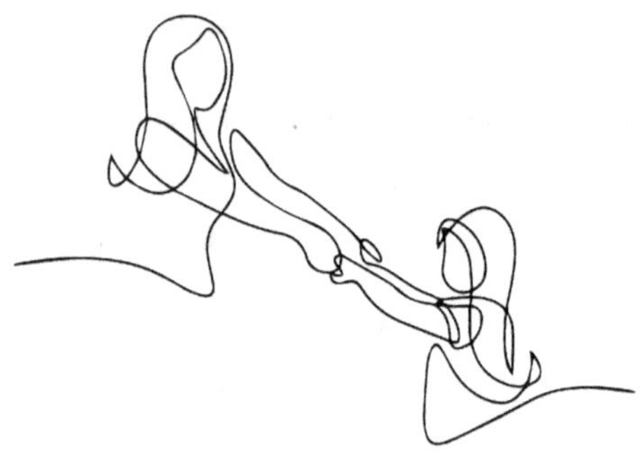

Here's to the woman who lit my way,
She gave me strength on the hardest days.
From the village paths to the halls of power,
She stood by me, every minute, every hour.

Her hands held mine when I was small,
She would lift me up with each stumble and
fall.
With fierce courage and gentle grace,
She helped me find my own true place.

She planted in me a seed of fire,
She led me forward, to dream and aspire.
Her words are like lamps in the darkest night,
Guiding my steps, filling my path with light.

In the soft whispers or words so strong,
She showed me where I truly belong.
She taught me that dreams are worth every
fight,
And her faith in me is my forever light.

So here I stand, with miles to go,
Filled with gratitude that will only grow,
For every moment you carried me through,
This journey, Mom, I owe it all to you.

In Every Morning, You Remain

Dear Dad,

I wake up before dawn in the still, quiet air,
remembering mornings, your calm presence
there.
Those 4 a.m. calls, so gentle and clear,
your voice, like a whisper, I still ache to hear.

I'd open my eyes to find you standing by,
with a peaceful smile, like morning's first
light.
You were my luck, my strength, my guide,
a steady warmth that made everything feel
right.

You called me your tigress, your fierce little
girl,
brave as a lion cub, the heart of your world.
With a laugh and a hug, you'd cheer me on,
I knew in your eyes I could do no wrong.

And those letters you wrote, I cherish each
line,
words full of love, gentle and kind.
Through pages worn, with edges frayed,
your voice is a melody that never fades.

So now, in these mornings when dawn feels
too far,
I close my eyes softly and know where you
are.
you live in the quiet, in the break of each day
guiding me gently, in your own way.

Though you're gone, you're never far,
You're still my morning, my guiding star.
And in my memory, you're here to stay,
a quiet light to guide my way.

This Beautiful Miracle

The moment I saw you,
my heart surrendered, falling deeply,
helplessly, true.
Maybe it seems like a fleeting thing,
but I'd defend it with every breath, every
string,
for you may be life's most beautiful design,
crafted with care, flawless and divine.

It's beyond my understanding, but maybe
God knew,
that my life would always be missing you,
a puzzle incomplete, a dream half-spun,
until our paths crossed, and we became the
one.

You're all the lovely things I cherish and see,
like poems, flowers, the pink dawn's plea,
a baby's laugh cradled close and warm.
I look at you and wonder in awe,
"What is this beautiful miracle that's come to
me?"

The Softest Heart

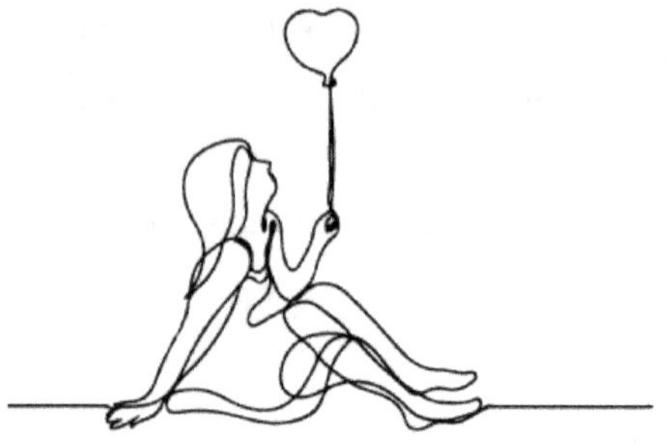

She wrote him poems, letters laced with her
soul,
poured out all the corners of her heart, whole.
She whispered, "No one's ever touched me
like this,
except the sunrays, the wind, and the rain's
gentle kiss."

She remembers when he promised her
forever,
but little did she know, his forever came with
terms and tether.
Now he looks past her, through her, cold as
stone,
as if her existence is a shadow, unknown.

So she builds a wall around her heart, brick
by aching brick,
hoping this fortress will finally stick.

She says, "The softest hearts bear the deepest
scars,"
and learns the truth, painful and hard.
Such experience is the teacher only few would
choose,
an unkind lesson in how much a good heart
can lose.

Ember Heart

She loves like an open road,
heart wide, hands steady, willing to go,
where others slow down, turn back,
her chest a map of small scars,
like stars too stubborn to fall.

She's a hopeless romantic,
and if her heart breaks, she calls it music.
She'll let it ache, slow and certain,
the way roots reach for soil they can't see,
but trust is there, waiting.

Last night, she whispered to the dark:
"I'd love again, even if it meant this."
and she meant it.
She is the kind to stitch hope to every empty
space.

Tomorrow, she'll wake, soft but unyielding,
her bruised heart like an ember,
still warm, still willing to burn.
She'll hold it out, gentle, knowing,
for someone else to see its glow.

She's learned that love is not for keeping,
but for giving, and giving again,
until one day, someone stays
long enough to call it home.

Longing for November

November is quiet,
just like a breath between seasons,
the wind speaks in whispers,
and the world slows its pace.
The days are short and the nights long,
the leaves fall without regret,
embracing the earth,
letting go of what they were.

There is something in the calm of autumn air,
a stillness that calls to me,
a space where the time is soft
and everything feels more certain
in its quiet decay.

All that feels just right.

I long to be like November,
not rushing, not chasing,
but simply being,
rooted in the present moment,
in the spaces between thoughts.
To stand like the trees,
letting go of what is no longer needed,
embracing the cold without fear.

I long to find strength in stillness,
in the knowing that what is lost
will make room for something new.

Where I Belong

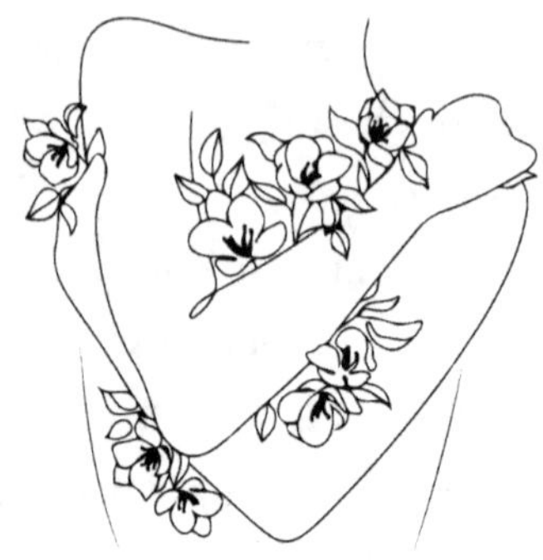

I have traveled through faces and voices,
through laughter and glances that faded like
smoke,
wandered dusty roads lined with stranger's
gaze,
I have known the ache of belonging nowhere.

But in you, I found a shelter,
just like the warmth that wraps around me,
a warm cozy blanket pulled close on the
coldest winter nights,
a place where my edges soften,
where the chill melts away.

When the world storms and I'm tossed by
waves,
your presence is the calm at the center,
the quiet eye in the hurricane,
where everything else falls silent,
and I, I breathe again.

You are made of pieces I recognize,
a kindness I met once, years ago,
the strength I saw in someone's hands,
the laughter of a friend who drifted away.
In you, they all return, stitched together
into a haven only you could be.

So, I rest here, wrapped in all that you are,
finding a home that grows deeper, softer,
with every heartbeat, every word unspoken,
a place where I am whole,
a place where I truly belong.

A Handful of Stars

I hold them in my palm,
these tiny lights that flicker
but do not burn.
They are my quiet wishes,
drifting through the vastness
of a night that never ends.

I have never learned
how to grasp what is so far away,
but my fingers ache
with the weight of what cannot be held.
Still, I try.
I hold these stars closer to my chest,
and for a moment,
the darkness feels less lonely.

There are days
when the sky seems too big to understand,
and I wonder if these stars
are just whispers of something lost,
a memory of light
that once shone brighter
but now lives only in the spaces between
heartbeats.

But even in their silence,
they remind me
there is beauty in longing,
in reaching for something that may never be
mine
and still, not letting go.

When the world feels too loud, too full,
I wrap my fingers around them,
hold them tight in my tiny arms,
and for a moment,
the chaos fades away.

I do not need to speak
to feel seen.
These handful of stars know
what I cannot say,
and I am happy
to let them glow,
in each corner
of my own heart.

Soft Revolutions

She does not shout,
but her silence is a protest
against all the words she was never allowed to
say.
Her stillness is not weakness,
but the quiet strength of a current
that moves unseen,
shaping the earth beneath her feet.

Each choice she makes
is an act of defiance,
small yet significant
She does not raise her fist,
she raises her head,
eyes clear,
not seeking permission to exist
but claiming her space
with every breath.

She walks through rooms
filled with expectations,
and does not bend to the shape of them.
Her body is a language of its own,
speaking in quiet gestures,
in the way she refuses to shrink,
even when the world tells her
to make herself smaller.

She does not need a revolution of fire,
but of soft, steady hands
that turn the wheel of change, one turn at a
time.

Her voice does not roar
but hums beneath the noise,
a song of resistance.

They do not see her revolt
not the bruises, not the scars,
but it is in the way she rises each day,
the way she loves
without losing herself,
the way she smiles
without apology,
the way she speaks her truth
into rooms that would rather remain silent.

And still, they do not understand
that this quiet force
is the one that will outlast them all.
A revolution,
soft, but relentless.

Unbound Unbroken

I walk away quietly,
when love falters, when the gaze turns cold.
The trees seem kinder, the wind more tender,
and I find myself in their arms, unbroken,
whole.
I leave not in anger, but in reverence for what
once was,
learning that some paths are meant to
diverge.

But I return, briefly,
not to linger, but to show the skies I have
healed.

Look, here I am; unburdened, unbound,
walking a different trail, yet standing tall.
I do not seek love, nor approval, nor light
from their sun.
I simply whisper to the silence: I'm doing fine.

Folded Pieces of a Tender Soul

I am the softest of hearts,
crying for stories I've never lived,
feeding love with every offering,
leaving whole worlds behind
for the warmth of familiar faces.
Words spill from my hands in quiet letters,
pieces of me folded into the pages.

And yet, I hide my storms,
lie to those who would carry my burdens,
if only to keep their skies clear.

Is it too much to hope for a world
where kindness walks openly,
where love is not a whispered rarity?
Why is kindness so rare?

A Letter to My Younger Self

Dear little one, with eyes cast low,
you hid your voice, let no one know
the dreams you held tightly in your tiny
hands,
it was the quiet strength that others could not
understand.

People laughed, at how you would speak and
stand,
they tried to pull you down and mocked the
ways of your village land.

You took those words and held them in your
heart tight,

but dear little one, I am glad you learned to
fight.

Your shyness that they could not see
was just a seed, waiting to rise patiently.
Your roots grew deep beneath their scorn,
for from that soil, you would be reborn.

I knew one day you would rise, stand firm
and true,
in the rooms where those same voices flew.
And now, they see a different face,
a self-made woman, grown, with quiet grace.

So, here's to you, the little girl I knew,
you faced storms and stayed so true.
You wore the mocking words like an armor of
steel,
And now, you are the proof that dreams can
heal.

The small village girl, so shy, so small,
would one day stand, so proud and tall.

Remember this whenever the doubts may grow:
You are much more than the naysayers, the whole world will know.

Dear Mr. Socrates

Dear Mr. Socrates,
you were one stubborn soul,
drinking poison yet standing firm,
unyielding in the face of death.
I always wonder what ran through your mind
in that final moment—
What made you believe that the truth you
gave up your life for
would spark a revolution of minds?

The dialogues you cherished,
The questions you lived for,
all lie buried beneath a crowd of loud and
hollow opinions.

We have forgotten that wisdom grows best
where doubt is allowed to bloom.

But I know somewhere in dusty books
or in the mind of a quiet seeker,
your spirit lingers, an echo, a spark,
an ember remains, wrapped in a corner of the
soul,
calling us back to the courage of asking,
to the quiet strength of seeking the ultimate
truth.

I meet myself once again

It's a quiet night in Havelock,
Stars are strewn like scattered silver
across the dark canvas of sky.
I walk barefoot along the shore,
where gentle waves kiss my feet,
each touch a whisper, soft and fleeting.

The white sand slips with every splash,
grain by grain, sifting through my toes.
I cling to it, holding tight,
as if my will alone could keep it still,
could stop time's slow retreat.

I don't want regrets, only to fight until the
last breath,
yet somewhere inside
there's a small, tired girl longing to rest in
gentle hands,
hands that will hold her just a little longer,
keeping her safe in their quiet warmth.

A gust of wind sweeps the grey clouds away,
clearing the sky, as if preparing itself for
dawn.
The first sunray reaches from the horizon,
and in that gentle glow, I meet myself once
again.
I met myself again!

9 789367 396148